40 KEYS

TO STAY REFRESHED

Methods for Keeping Yourself Renewed and Invigorated

Author
CHERLENE ADEWUNMI

INTRODUCTION

Imagine accessing *40 powerful keys* that open doors to a more fulfilling life.

Unlock your spirit and enhance your life with **"40 Keys to Stay Refreshed."** This is a refreshing dip into the wellspring of the Holy Spirit, designed to nourish your mind, body, and spirit.

Each key serves as a reminder that you possess the power to transform your life.

For each key, take a moment to meditate on it. Decide what you need to do with each key to gain access to new levels of living Refreshed.

Refresh your spirit and embrace the new journey that lies ahead!

LOVE GOD

You shall love the Lord your God with all your heart and with all your soul and with all your might. Deuteronomy 6:5

This verse is part of the Shema, a key declaration of faith for the Israelites. Loving God isn't just about feelings; it's a total commitment that involves your heart (your emotions and will), your soul (your essence and spirit), and your might (your strength and actions).

What does it mean to actually love God? It's more than just saying the words or attending church services. It's about building an intimate relationship with the Holy Spirit who is God. This means spending time in prayer, reading the Bible, and seeking to understand the character of the Holy Spirit and the will for your life. It's about trust, that even when life gets tough, you will make the right choices that reflect God's character.

If you truly love someone, you want to honor them and align your actions with what matters to them. Loving God means living a life that reflects God's commands.

TRUST GOD

The Holy Spirit is God, our Advocate and Helper. The Holy Spirit is here to guide our lives.

For those who are led by the Spirit of God are the children of God. **Romans 8:14**

Trusting the Holy Spirit means being led in all decisions, big or small. It's about praying for direction before making decisions.

LIVE FOR GOD

Therefore, I urge you, brothers and sisters, in view of God's mercy, to offer your bodies as a living sacrifice, holy and pleasing to God—this is your true and proper worship. **Romans 12:1**

Living for God looks like acts of kindness, serving others, standing up for what is right, and sharing the love of God everywhere.

FORGIVE OTHERS

For if you forgive other people when they sin against you, your heavenly Father will also forgive you. But if you do not forgive others their sins, God will not forgive your sins. **Matthew 6:14-15**

Forgiving others means letting go of all offenses and ill will. If you want to be refreshed every day, make it a habit to forgive daily!

FORGIVE YOURSELF

If we confess our sins, God is faithful and just and will forgive us our sins and purify us from all unrighteousness. 1 John 1:9

When you sincerely seek forgiveness from God, a change of heart and action happens. Just asking for forgiveness without a commitment to transform won't free you from the consequences of your actions. Seeking forgiveness means committing to a covenant relationship with the Holy Spirit.

RELEASE BITTERNESS

Bitterness is resentment. It steals your peace and joy, and it thrives in a heart void of God. No matter how much you try to hide it, bitterness will ruin your body, your life, and every relationship you have. It is poison that seeps into you and affects everyone around you, especially those you love.

Ephesians 4:31-32 commands you to **get rid of all bitterness, rage, and anger, and instead be kind, compassionate, and forgiving.**

EMBRACE JOY

Joy is a secured state of being for those who are anchored in the Holy Spirit.

The joy of the Lord is your strength. Nehemiah 8:10

Rejoice in the Lord always: and again I say, Rejoice.

Let your moderation be known unto all men. The Lord is at hand.

Be careful for nothing; but in everything by prayer and supplication with thanksgiving let your requests be made known unto God.

And the peace of God, which passeth all understanding, shall keep your hearts and minds through Christ Jesus.

Finally, brethren, whatsoever things are true, whatsoever things are honest, whatsoever things are just, whatsoever things are pure, whatsoever things are lovely, whatsoever things are of good report; if there be any virtue, and if there be any praise, think on these things. Philippians 4:4-8

A LIFE WITH GOD

Those who are led by the Spirit of God are the children of God. Romans 8:14

Revelation 21:4 paints a beautiful picture of what's in store for God's chosen: ***"God will wipe every tear from their eyes. There will be no more death or mourning or crying or pain. "*** The ultimate reward is eternal life here on earth with God, in a land flowing with milk and honey.

PRAISE AND WORSHIP

Enter God's gates with thanksgiving and the inner courts with praise and thanksgiving. Psalm 100:4

Praise involves your whole being—your mind, your voice, body, heart, and spirit. It is a magnanimous celebration of God.

Worship is honoring the presence and work of the Holy Spirit in your life and the world.

Worshiping the Holy Spirit means living a life filled with prayer and praise, and reflecting the fruits of the Holy Spirit— love, joy, peace, and kindness.

ESTABLISH A RELATIONSHIP WITH THE HOLY SPIRIT

Establishing a relationship with the Holy Spirit is the only way to life. The Holy Spirit is God.

The Holy Spirit will guide us into all truth. **John 16:13**

To listen is to obey.

Spending quality time with the Holy Spirit daily—through prayer, meditation, and quiet reflection—is the key to a glorious life.

DO WHAT THE HOLY SPIRIT TELLS YOU TO DO

If you reason with an arrogant cynic, you'll get slapped in the face; confront bad behavior and get a kick in the shins. So don't waste your time on a scoffer; all you'll get for your pain is abuse. But if you correct those who care about life, that's different—they'll love you for it! Save your breath for the wise- they'll be wiser for it; tell good people what you know—they'll profit from it. Skilled living gets its start in the Fear-of-GOD, insight into life from knowing a Holy God. It's through me, Lady Wisdom, that your life deepens, and the years of your life ripen. Live wisely and wisdom will permeate your life; mock life and life will mock you. Proverbs 9:7-12

THE HOLY SPIRIT WILL SHOW YOU WHO YOU ARE

We are God's handiwork, created for good works prepared in advance for us to do. **Ephesians 2:10**

Embrace your identity and purpose, so that you do not miss out on God.

THE HOLY SPIRIT WILL SHOW YOU YOUR PURPOSE

For I know the plans I have for you, declares the Lord, plans to prosper you and not to harm you, plans to give you hope and a future. Jeremiah 29:11

For we are God's handiwork, created in Christ Jesus to do good works, which God prepared in advance for us to do. Ephesians 2:10

THE HOLY SPIRIT WILL TEACH YOU

In the Gospel of John, chapter 14, verse 26. Jesus is speaking to his disciples during the Last Supper, preparing them for his impending departure. He promises that after he leaves, God will come to guide them, and help them understand the truths of faith.

This promise is significant and highlights the role of the Holy Spirit, the only Teacher, the only God.

THE HOLY SPIRIT WILL RESTORE ALL THINGS

From the very beginning, the Bible tells us how God created the world and everything in it, declaring it "very good" (Genesis 1:31). But then humanity chose its own path, leading to a separation from God and a distortion of that original goodness.

The old has passed away; the new has come. 2 Corinthians 5:17

The Holy Spirit is restoring all things! This includes the earth, everything in it, humanity, and the universe.

THE HOLY SPIRIT WILL SHOW YOU THE TRUE MEANING OF LIFE

Eternal life is more than living forever; it's about a standard of living that starts now and continues beyond the current physical existence.

Now this is eternal life: that they know you, the only true God. John 17:3

Life begins with a personal relationship with the Holy Spirit.

THE HOLY SPIRIT BRINGS JOY
AND PEACE

"But the fruit of the Spirit is love, joy, peace, patience, kindness, goodness, faithfulness, gentleness, self-control; against such things there is no law". Galatians 5:22-23

May the God of hope fill you with all joy and peace as you trust in him, so that you may overflow with hope by the power of the Holy Spirit. Romans 15:13

THE HOLY SPIRIT BRINGS LOVE

The Holy Spirit is God, The Comforter, The Only Guide, and Helper.

Dear friends, let us love one another, for love comes from God. Everyone who loves has been born of God and knows God. Whoever does not love does not know God, because God is love. 1 John 4:7-8

MENTAL CAPACITY

Do not conform to the pattern of this world but be transformed by the renewing of your mind. Romans 12:2

The more you challenge your thinking, the more you grow.

A double minded man is unstable in all his ways James 1:8

STUDY THE BIBLE

When you take the time to study biblical wisdom and apply it to your lives, we will find ourselves leading healthier, happier lives.

For the word of God is quick, and powerful, and sharper than any two-edged sword, piercing even to the dividing asunder of soul and spirit, and of the joints and marrow, and is a discerner of the thoughts and intents of the heart. Hebrews 4:11

Let us labor therefore to enter into that rest, lest any man fall after the same example of unbelief. Hebrews 4:12

MEDITATE ON GOD

Think about things that are true, noble, right, pure, lovely, and admirable. Philippians 4:8

Meditation is prayer.

Do not be anxious about anything. Instead, present your requests to God through prayer and supplication, all while being thankful. Philippians 4:6

Whatever is true - Start with honesty. Embrace the reality around you and avoid getting caught up in lies or misinformation.

Whatever is noble – Think about things that are dignified and honorable.

Whatever is right – Make ethical decisions.

Whatever is pure - Meditate on things that are wholesome and clean.

Whatever is lovely – Find joy in the beauty of nature.

Whatever is admirable – Reflect on qualities and actions that inspire respect.

If anything is excellent or praiseworthy – Seek out what's truly remarkable by God's standards and rejoice in God. God is great and worthy of all praise!

By keeping these thoughts in mind, you can create a more positive and fulfilling mental space.

STAY FOCUSED ON LIVING A HEALTHY LIFE

Do you not know that your body is a temple of the Holy Spirit? You are not your own; you were bought at a price. Therefore, honor God with your bodies. 1 Corinthians 6:19-20

Take care of yourselves in a way that honors God, recognizing the gift of life and health you've been given. Living a healthy life includes nurturing your spiritual, physical, mental, and emotional well-being.

ESTABLISH A LIFE OF PRAYER

Prayer is your direct communication with the Holy Spirit.

LIMIT TELEVISION

Above all else, guard your heart, for everything you do flows from it. Proverbs 4:23

LIMIT SOCIAL MEDIA

Do not be deceived: Bad company corrupts good morals. 1 Corinthians 15:33

SET BOUNDARIES

Do not set foot on the path of the wicked or walk in the way of evildoers. Proverbs 4:14

Test everything by the Holy Spirit.

STAY AWAY FROM TOXIC PEOPLE

Blessed is the individual who walketh not in the counsel of the ungodly, nor standeth in the way of sinners, nor sitteth in the seat of the scornful.

But his delight is in the law of the Lord; and in his law doth he meditate day and night. And he shall be like a tree planted by the rivers of water, that bringeth forth his fruit in his season; his leaf also shall not wither; and whatsoever he doeth shall prosper. Psalms 1:1-3

FOCUS ON YOU

Live a life of high moral standards and stay productive.

Keep your focus on your own journey and responsibilities—don't get caught up in what others are doing.

COMMIT YOUR WORKS UNTO GOD

Commit your work unto God, and God's plans will be established in your life. Proverbs 16:3

CELEBACY AND ABSTINENCE

Abstain from sexual relations until your covenant marriage.

Building an intimate covenant relationship with the Holy Spirit before marriage sets the stage for a strong marital bond — just be sure to keep your relationship with God as your top priority.

Thou shalt have no other gods before me. Thou shalt not make unto thee any graven image, or any likeness *of anything* that *is* in heaven above, or that *is* in the earth beneath, or that *is* in the water under the earth: thou shalt not bow down thyself to them, nor serve them: for I the Lord thy God *am* a jealous God, visiting the iniquity of the fathers upon the children unto the third and fourth *generation* of them that hate me. Exodus 20:3-5

INTIMACY WITH GOD COMES FIRST

For any marriage to thrive, each person must have a covenant relationship with the Holy Spirit. This intimacy with God is non- negotiable; it's the bedrock for a successful marriage.

When you draw near to God, God will draw near to you. James 4:8

When both partners prioritize their relationship with the Holy Spirit, their marriage is filled with love, grace, mercy, patience, kindness, hospitality, forgiveness, power, purity, honor, integrity, holiness, understanding, and abundant life.

REST

Make time to refresh yourself; it's not a luxury, it's a necessity. Take daily and weekly times of rest and refreshing without distractions.

God blessed the seventh day and made it holy and rested. Genesis 2:3

AVOID CONFRONTATION

Blessed are the peacemakers, for they are the children of God. Matthew 5:9

A soft answer turns away wrath, but a harsh word stirs up anger. Proverbs 15:1

Blessed are the meek, for they shall inherit the earth. Matthew 5:5

SPEAK LIFE

Death and life are in the power of the tongue, and those who love it will eat its fruits. Proverbs 18:21

Do not let any unwholesome talk come out of your mouths, but only what is helpful for building others up according to their needs, that it may benefit you and those who listen. Ephesians 4:29

CREATE THE PLACE FOR GOD

Be still and know that I am God. Psalms 46:10

Create a quiet space where you can be alone with God, free from distractions. It is in the solitude of this place that you can truly connect with the Holy Spirit and discover your life's will and purpose.

THE HOUSE OF GOD

Make your house a place where everyone who walks in can feel God's presence—a home that is clean and orderly.

ESTABLISH THE ATMOSPHERE FOR GOD

The peace that only God provides surpasses all understanding. Philippians 4:7

Creating a peaceful and clean atmosphere at home is more than tidiness; it is where tranquility and harmony reside.

THE APPETITE LIKE THE HOLY SPIRIT

So, I say this: Walk in the Spirit, and you won't fulfill the desires of the flesh.

For the flesh desires what is contrary to the Holy Spirit, and the Holy Spirit desires what is contrary to the flesh. They're in conflict with each other, so you can't do what you want to do.

But if you're led by the Holy Spirit, you're not under the law.

Now, the acts of the flesh are obvious: they include adultery, fornication, uncleanness, and lasciviousness.

Also, there's idolatry, witchcraft, hatred, discord, jealousy, anger, strife, divisions, and heresies.

Then there are envy, murder, drunkenness, and partying—along with similar things. I'm telling you this ahead of time, as I've mentioned before, that those who practice such things won't inherit the kingdom of God. Galatians 5:16-21

AVOID EXCESS

If you find honey, eat just enough—too much of it, and you will vomit. Proverbs 24:16

Wine is a mocker, strong drink is raging: and whosoever is deceived thereby is not wise. Proverbs 20:1

Not that I am speaking of being in need, for I have learned in whatever situation I am to be content.

I know how to be brought low, and I know how to abound. In any and every circumstance, I have learned the secret of facing plenty and hunger, abundance and need. I can do all things through God who strengthens me. Philippians 4:11-13

TAKE LEISURE WALKS

Enoch walked faithfully with God; then he was no more, because God took him away. Genesis 5:24

Life is all about our relationship with the Holy Spirit! When we make the effort to walk with God, we can then dwell with God.

www.ingramcontent.com/pod-product-compliance
Lightning Source LLC
Chambersburg PA
CBHW071243090426
42736CB00014B/3202